Maya's Book of Poems

Karamjit Ram

Contents

Dedication

I dedicate this book to my nieces and nephews, who are also my inspiration for writing this book. I would like to thank my parents for their good upbringing and for allowing me to freely develop in order for me to write.

I would like to thank my siblings for their continued support throughout my life.

Acknowledgements

I would like to thank my team at American Publishers Inc. for their hard work and dedication in bringing this book to life.

From editorial to design, to production, your efforts have been appreciated. Thank you for your support throughout this process.

Karamjit

About the Author

Born in the UK in the 1970s to Hindu Punjabi parents originally from Punjab, India, Karamjit has built a diverse career grounded in both professional and creative pursuits. A graduate of the University of Warwick and Wolverhampton University, she has worked across multiple industries, bringing a wealth of experience to each role.

In addition to her professional achievements, Karamjit is a classically trained musician. She continues to nurture this passion through ongoing adult tutorship, maintaining a high level of skill and dedication to the art.

Section One

New Home

Clutter, bang, pack, move
Clunk, clunk, clunk
In goes all that belongs
To a car that goes with a bang

A pang of earnest grows
A change as fears grow
To pastures new
With delicate views
And doubtful news

The interior, new but subtle
To the eye, as far as one can see
A change, with a back garden's view
Through a window ledge
Showing the tree of fruit
Which looms in the midst of dwelling's new.

Karamjit Ram

Starting School

Toys are new
A colourful muse
In go the shapes
Out come the capes

Drawers are plenty
The floor is empty
And chairs to sit
With a burning grip

To learn what is new
With a spirit bursting with enlightenment
Person to person
Character to character

Looms a willingness
To see faces anew
Colour, creations, and ambitions too.

Baby Pets

Baby pets are all the rage
Both are all on one page
The noise of the animals sounds
With the pounding of one's playful paws

Jaws sharp as blades
Looking to create a scene
Slippers in tatters
And balls pounced upon

Pet couches all the rage
Sleeping without due rest
And all is to play for
With no fear in sight
And a night to prey.

Karamjit Ram

New Neighbours

Long hair and braids
Shows girly parades
Skirts and shirts
Dress-up days

Boxes and bins aplenty
Amidst the clutter
Creation of jumbles of sales
Dolls, fashionista and new
Become idols of the few

Today is tomorrow
And the next another age
Beauty shines, faces alight
With delights all around.

School Hols

The sun is bright
Filled with hearts' delight
The sand is warm
As friends alight with joy

Endeavours new
Fun are the days
The wayward ways
Of little beings

Soaking up fish delights
In open air and a gentle sea breeze
Which dulls the heated air
And rises up above to release a sweat.

Winter's New

As she strides through the leafy grass
Bold as brass
Cold as she might be in an autumn breeze
Next will be the winter freeze
Piled high, the winter's snow

Out in the open air
One has to compare
From winters past
Which were made to last

The change of times
Swindled change of crime of weather's new
With rain so fast, with downpours to last.

End of Section One

Section Two

Destined Plight

Destined as through life,
A plight of pleasure
With the sound of a gun,
A shroud of hummingbirds.
Is this the bird of paradise?

The shadow before you
Shows a trick,
And with such luck,
You will get the answer
To a destined sum.

Hapless is a stranger,
Yet unknown to danger;
But he proceeds
Not as a stranger,
For fortune, as he is destined to loot.

With the sound of a gun,
As the bird of paradise is destined through plight.

Oyster Parade

Oyster Parade of love,
Take the rest of my life,
My revelations,
My heart falling,
My conscience is reserved.

The way of the sun
At the end of the day,
Night always comes,
Pursuing the truth,
The way of the world,
An oyster parade.

The way of her smile,
Her eyes that burn with envy,
The cycle of life,
Seasonal change,
An oyster parade.

Masterful Deceit

Deceit is masterful,
Insistent, demanding,
In the spotlight,
So, in control,
A face to unmask.

A second's impression is lost,
Briefest of glimpses,
Insecurities obscured from mind.

Be afraid, as this is your life.
I used to live such whiles,
Hiding behind the curtain, waiting to fall.
Your face, quietly confident,
You approach, almost as a master of deceit.

Solitaire

Play it hard, play it fast,
Play it cool, play it sweet,
As soon as you give the game away.

Don't give it all;
Let her sense the need.
You've got to take the lead,
Gotta go easy to achieve.
Pick up the phone,
Gotta get her alone.

If you lose control,
You will not be the first or the last.
You will never see me turn around.
Solitaire, Solitaire.

Karamjit Ram

Loyal Patron

I see the spirit moving,
Loyal patron.

See the power in your hand;
Keep both feet firmly planted on the ground.
I have found to wrestle with eternal questions.
It breaks my heart—
Your alluring eyes,
That quest to move my life.

I would draw you in my heart
If your eyes were not closed to me.
I would draw you as my world
If I could speak my mind.

Secret places to find,
Your spirit longs to breathe.
Souls wander in the sand, unaware.
Take my hand in the desert heat,
For I am your loyal patron.

Karamjit Ram

Honour of Evils

Honour of evils,
Cover my weakness.
Try with all my might
To fight my battles.

Seize the day; got to be right.
You are my one true spirit—
Gotta be right,
Breakthrough light.

Loneliness plays the darkness,
Caressing my vengefulness.
You conquer me every time,
Mending broken hearts.

Look up and face the deepest fears
That shade us from the fiery heat
And bows that strike—
Honour amongst evils' plights.

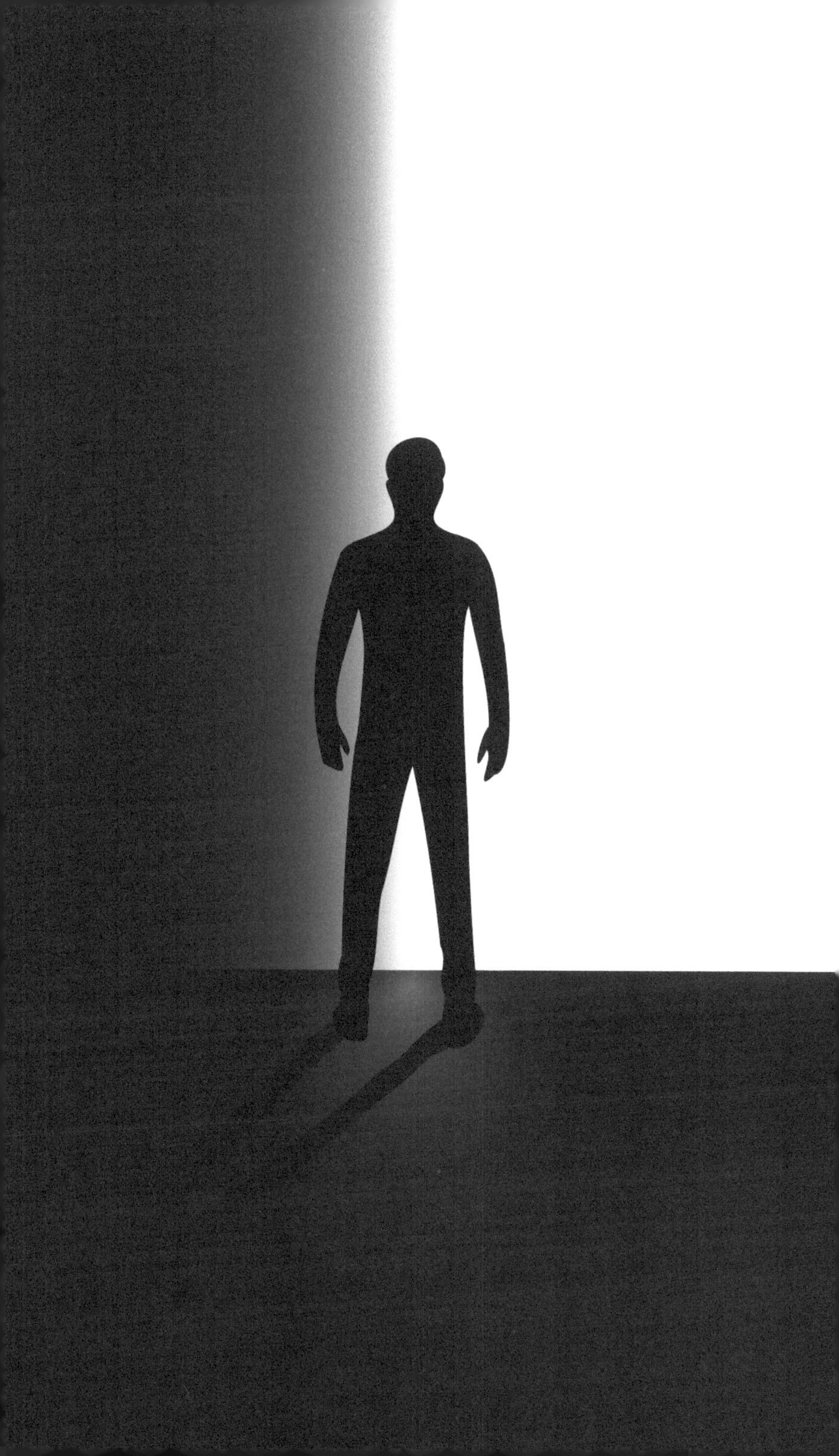

Karamjit Ram

Majestic Duty

Majestic calls to the known,
Duty above all that is dear;
So, I shall lay my life
For duty calls its majestic hand.

I shall discover what you
Must hide,
For I am not divine of a dutiful challenge.

As majestic are my deeds,
I follow my aim to its end
As duty calls its majestic hand.

Karamjit Ram

Changra (Noise)

Loudness of the changra
Shows strength for the weak.
The silence of the night
Shows shadows alight.

As the day dawns,
Mists arise—no evil
Or gladness in sight.
For the lessoned changra
Of idylls alight with a ploy.

But play as the night fades;
The changra weakens
Like a silenced eclipse in the night.
The shadows' gladness arise
As the changra draws to an end.

The silence of the night
Shows shadows alight.
The changra weakens
Like an eclipse in the night.
As the night fades, the changra ends.